Listening Tasks

For Intermediate Students of American English

Student's Book

Sandra Schecter, adapter

Based on *Task Listening* by
Lesley Blundell and Jackie Stokes

Adapted from *Listening Tasks* by Lesley Blundell and Jackie Stokes (Cambridge: Cambridge University Press, 1981).

Published by the Press Syndicate of the University of Cambridge
The Pitt Building, Trumpington Street, Cambridge CB2 IRP
40 West 20th Street, New York, NY 10011-4211, USA
10 Stamford Road, Oakleigh, Melbourne 3166, Australia

© Cambridge University Press 1984

First published 1984
Eighth printing 1995

Printed in the United States of America

Library of Congress Cataloging-in-Publication Data is available.

A catalog record for this book is available from the British Library.

ISBN 0-521-27898-8 Student's Book
ISBN 0-521-27897-X Teacher's Manual
ISBN 0-521-26258-5 Cassette

Contents

Acknowledgments   v

Introduction   1

1   **Using a bank**   2
2   **Following instructions about a sport**   4
3   **Leaving a message**   6
4   **Catching planes and trains**   8
5   **Checking on hotel facilities**   10
6   **Being a good observer**   12
7   **Watching the weather**   14
8   **Apartment hunting**   16
9   **Finding out what's going on in town**   18
10   **Finding out about a course**   20
11   **Talking about television**   22
12   **Running errands**   24
13   **Phoning a service station**   26
14   **Moving in**   28
15   **Handling an emergency**   30
16   **Making travel plans**   32
17   **Renting a car**   34
18   **Fitting in an appointment**   36
19   **Learning how to use a machine**   38
20   **Sightseeing**   40

Acknowledgments

The author and publisher are grateful to the following for permission to reproduce illustrations and photographs: VISA U.S.A. and Chase Manhattan Bank (p. 3); News and Publications Service, Stanford University: gymnastics (p. 3); Tim Davis Photography: tennis and track (p. 4); Maggie Stocking: diver (p. 4); American Airlines: surfer (p. 4); Jack Graham: swimmer (p. 4); YWCA of New York City (p. 5); New Jersey Transit Corporation (p. 9); Larry Anger (p. 12); AP/Wide World Photos: frontiertown (p. 13); The San Francisco Examiner: "On Strike" and "Bob's Used Cars" (p. 13); United Press Canada: "Women against Pornography" (p. 13); Punch Publications Ltd.: cartoon by Raymonde (top right, p. 15); Lucasfilm Ltd.: *The Empire Strikes Back*, © 1980 Lucasfilm Ltd. (p. 18); United Artists: *Casablanca*, © 1943 Warner Bros. Pictures, Inc., renewed 1970 United Artists Television, Inc. (p. 18), photograph from the Museum of Modern Art/ Film Stills Archive; United Artists: *Rocky III*, © 1982 United Artists Corporation; Columbia Pictures: *Kramer vs. Kramer*, photograph from the Museum of Modern Art/Film Stills Archive; San Francisco Symphony: Beethoven advertisement (p. 19); Lorimar Production Inc.: "Dallas," TM & © 1984 Lorimar Production Inc. (p. 22); Universal Pictures: *The Bride of Frankenstein*, 1935 (p. 22); The National Broadcasting Company, Inc.: Connie Chung (p. 22); Spartan Sports Service, Michigan State University (p. 22); White Rose Food Corporation (p. 25); Lindsay Olive Growers (p. 25); Amstar Corporation: Domino® Sugar (Domino® is the registered trademark of Amstar Corporation) (p. 25); The Coca-Cola Company (p. 25); The Proctor & Gamble Company: Ivory Soap (p. 25); American Motors Corporation: Jeep Cherokee (p. 27); Chrysler Corporation: Dodge Aries (p. 27); Toyota Motor Sales, U.S.A., Inc. (p. 27); Chevrolet Division of General Motors Corp. (p. 27); General Electric (p. 29); St. John Ambulance, Canada (p. 30); Master Eagle Gallery: photograph by Kam Mak (p. 31); Hyatt Hotels Corporation (p. 33); California Office of Tourism, Sacramento (p. 33); Washington Convention and Visitors Association: photographs (p. 40).

Illustrations by Tom Ickert: pages 6, 8, 10, 15 (bottom left and right), 32

Cover design by Frederick Charles Ltd.
Book design by Peter Ducker
Layout by Publishers' Graphics
Cassette production by The Sun Group

Introduction

Listening Tasks helps make listening to English easy!

You may find it difficult to understand English spoken at normal speed because it seems too fast, and the language you have already learned may seem incomprehensible when used in everyday conversation. These problems arise because you are probably trying to catch every word and are missing the overall message as a result. *Listening Tasks* will help you to listen for the *substance* of what someone is saying and to pick out the information you really need to know.

Listening Tasks consists of twenty units. In each unit you will hear a short recording and do a practical exercise in your book, such as labeling a picture or filling in a chart. The recordings are of people speaking at normal speed in everyday situations. Each unit has as its theme a setting or situation in which listening plays a major part, for example, listening for flight announcements at an airport or asking about different courses available at a college.

When you listen to the recording, remember that you do not need to understand every single word to get the general idea of what is being said and to do the task. For example, in Unit 1, "Using a bank" (page 2), there is a blank check. The setting for the recording is a bank, where a cashier is helping a customer write a check. The task for you is to do just that – write a check. You may listen to the tape as many times as you want in order to get all the relevant details to complete the task.

In addition to the listening task, there are also reading and writing tasks related to the theme of the unit. So, for example, after filling in the check in Unit 1, you are asked to look at a month's bills and to fill in a deposit slip for the amount of those bills. Sometimes you are asked to do a lengthier writing task – a postcard to a friend or instructions on how to run a machine, for instance. Wherever a longer piece of writing is called for, you will probably want to use a separate page rather than write in your Student's Book.

If you are using the book for self-study rather than as a class text, you may want to consult the Teacher's Manual, which contains the tapescripts and answers to all the tasks.

1 Using a bank

Dan is in a bank and wants to get some money. Listen to his conversation with the bank teller and fill in the blank check.

DANIEL KIRKLAND
4091 Deerwood Lane
Minneapolis, MN 55441

100

_____ 19 _____

PAY TO THE
ORDER OF _____ $ [   ]

_____ D O L L A R S

Metro North Savings Bank
54 North Avenue
Minneapolis, Minnesota 55436

MEMO _____   _____

⑂100 ⑊ 48 ⑊44 8⑊

Nick Arnopoulos is paying his monthly bills. He wants to deposit enough money to cover the total amount of these bills and have $10 left in his checking account. Fill in the deposit slip.

CHASE MANHATTAN *VISA*®

The Chase Manhattan Bank, N.A.

Make check or money order payable to CHASE VISA. Payment must be made in U.S. dollars.

NICK ARNOPOULOS
109 OAK STREET
APT. 2
CLINTON, MA 01510

Please indicate any change of name and address here

12/28	4225 900 100 111	195.00	10.00	
STATEMENT CLOSING DATE	ACCOUNT NUMBER	TOTAL NEW BALANCE	MINIMUM DUE THIS BILLING	AMOUNT ENCLOSED

Return this portion of statement with payment. Our address on back must show in window of enclosed envelope.

ON GAS

	AMOUNT
	32.75
	.12
TOTAL CURRENT CHARGES	32.87
PREVIOUS BALANCE	38.88
12/10 CREDIT	38.88
TOTAL AMOUNT NOW DUE	$32.87

WALTER MOODY, M.D.
30 ELM AVENUE
CLINTON, MASSACHUSETTS 01510

To Nick Arnopoulos
For professional services rendered:

Physical examination 12/15

Office visit..............................$50.00
X-rays....................................$30.00
Blood tests...............................$25.00
Total due................................$105.00

DEPOSIT SLIP

NICK ARNOPOULOS
109 Oak St., #2
Clinton, MA 01510

DATE _____ 19 _____

CASH		
LIST CHECKS SINGLY		
TOTAL		

BE SURE EACH ITEM IS PROPERLY ENDORSED

National Bank
& TRUST COMPANY
333 JEFFERSON AVENUE, CLINTON, MA 01510

101 ⑈ 13650 6⑈

3

2 Following instructions about a sport

Which sport is being taught? Put a check (√) in the box below the correct photo. Make a list of the important words that helped you reach this conclusion.

Gymnastics ☐

Tennis ☐

Jogging ☐

Diving ☐

Surfing ☐

Swimming ☐

1

2

3

4

Match three of the pictures with the instructions by writing the correct numbers in the boxes below. Then write instructions to go with the other picture.

☐   A. Sit on the floor with your legs straight in front of you. Stretch your arms forward and touch your toes.

☐   B. Lie on your back. Lift your legs straight up and point your toes. Then lift your hips off the floor. Support yourself with your hands on your lower back.

☐   C. Sit cross-legged. Raise your right arm over your head and stretch to the left.

☐   D.

3   Leaving a message

A woman is trying to phone her friend. Put a check (√) next to the
picture that best describes the message that she leaves.

Where would you expect to see these notes, notices, or signs?

Passengers needed for carpool. Lexington to Boston.

Leave 7 a.m., return 5 pm.

Evelyn (617)-782-5948 (eve.)

STRIKE

Attractive, athletic male, single, 25 yrs., loves good food, wine, music, and stimulating conversation. Seeks Miss Right for honest, open relationship. Box 1907.

Terry —
Gone to work!
Milk + leftovers
in refrigerator.
See you later.
— Tony

STOP

NO TRESPASSING

CLOSED

Be back
in

10

min.

You have to go out for half an hour. Write a message to put on your door for a guest who is arriving today.

4 Catching planes and trains

Announcements are coming over the loudspeaker in an airport.
What are the travelers saying? Fill in the missing information.

Choose a train for Sarah to take and complete her postcard to George and Jenny.

45 Melrose Ave.
Newark, NJ 07106

Dear Sarah,
So glad you're coming to visit! Why don't you take a Saturday morning train — you can catch one at the Penn Center Philadelphia terminal, can't you?
If you get to Newark by noon we can go out for lunch. Write and let us know when your train gets in — we'll pick you up at the station.
Love,
George & Jenny

NJ TRANSIT

Saturdays

Train No.	A 66	7800	7802	A 252	7700	A 198	7804	3250	A 168	A 44	7702	A 182	7806	A 170	3252	7704	A 20	7808	A 174
	A.M.	A.M.	A.M.	A.M.	A.M.	A.M.	A.M.	A.M.	A.M.	A.M.	A.M.	A.M.	A.M.	A.M.	A.M.	A.M.	A.M.	A.M.	P.M.
Penn Center, Phila.	—	....	....	—	....	—	7.15	....	—	—	....	—	9.15	—	....	....	—	11.15	—
30th St. Station	12.57	....	....	6.50	....	7.25	7.18	....	8.46	9.10	....	9.28	9.18	10.25	....	....	11.31	11.18	12.27
North Phila.	—	....	....	6.59	....	7.34	7.26	....	—	9.19	....	—	9.26	—	....	....	—	11.26	—
Trenton (SEPTA)	—	....	....	—	....	—	8.10	....	—	—	....	—	—	—	....	....	—	12.10	—
Trenton, N.J.	1.28	5.30	6.30	7.22	....	8.00	8.30	....	9.18	9.41	....	9.58	10.30	10.55	....	....	12.05	12.30	12.57
Princeton Jct. S	—	5.40	6.40	—	....	8.09	8.40	....	—	9.49	....	—	10.40	—	....	....	—	12.40	—
Jersey Avenue	—	—	—	—	7.50	—	—	....	—	—	9.50	—	—	—	....	11.50	—	—	—
New Brunswick	—	5.55	6.55	—	7.55	8.21	8.55	....	—	10.02	9.55	—	10.55	—	....	11.55	—	12.55	—
Edison	—	5.58	6.58	—	7.58	—	8.58	....	—	—	9.58	—	10.58	—	....	11.58	—	12.58	—
Metuchen	—	6.02	7.02	—	8.02	—	9.02	....	—	—	10.02	—	11.02	—	....	12.02	—	1.02	—
Metro Park (Iselin)	1.53	6.06	7.06	—	8.06	8.30	9.06	....	9.42	—	10.06	—	11.06	11.20	....	12.06	—	1.06	—
Rahway	—	6.10	7.10	—	8.10	—	9.10	9.39	—	—	10.10	—	11.10	—	11.39	12.10	—	1.10	—
North Rahway	—	—	—	—	—	—	—	—	—	—	—	—	—	—	—	—	—	—	—
Linden	—	6.14	7.14	—	8.14	—	9.14	9.43	—	—	10.14	—	11.14	—	11.43	12.14	—	1.41	—
Elizabeth	—	6.19	7.19	—	8.19	—	9.19	9.48	—	—	10.19	—	11.19	—	11.48	12.19	—	1.19	—
North Elizabeth	—	—	7.21	—	8.21	—	9.21	—	—	—	—	—	—	—	—	—	—	—	—
Newark, N.J. P	2.19	6.26	7.27	7.58	8.27	8.50	9.27	9.55	10.05	10.24	10.26	D10.36	11.26	11.38	11.55	12.26	D12.45	1.26	1.32
New York, N.Y.	2.35	6.43	7.44	8.14	8.44	9.06	9.42	10.10	10.16	10.40	10.43	10.52	11.41	11.54	12.12	12.43	1.00	1.43	1.47

Dear George and Jenny,
Thanks _____.
I _____ from Penn Center at _____ so I _____ in Newark at _____.
Love,
Sarah

George & Jenny Fulton
45 Melrose Ave.
Newark, N.J. 07106

9

5   Checking on hotel facilities

A bellhop is taking a hotel guest to her room. Check (√) each hotel facility or service that is available and make brief notes about its location, if mentioned.

1607

Facility	Available	Location
TV		
radio		
restaurant		
coffee shop		
parking		
room service		
conference rooms		
cocktail lounge		
bell captain		
swimming pool		

Read the notice posted for hotel guests and answer the questions about checking out.

GH

Grand Hotel
Room 1067
Rate for one person $50.00
Rate for two persons $65.00

When Checking Out
1. Check out by 12:00 noon.
2. Be sure to take all your personal belongings.
3. Leave your key at the front desk.
4. Ask for your bill and pay at the cashier's desk. Personal checks are not accepted.

In Case of Fire
1. Go to nearest FIRE ALARM BOX and pull alarm. Fire extinguishers are available next to each FIRE ALARM BOX.
2. Do not use elevators.
3. Follow signs to the nearest EMERGENCY EXIT in order to evacuate the building.

IMPORTANT: Emergency exits are marked with red lights. Please familiarize yourself with the location of the exit nearest this room.

When checking out:
Can I leave my room after 12 p.m.?

_____

Where do I get my bill? _____

_____

My bill for 4 nights (one person)

comes to _____

Can I pay by check? _____

1061   EMERGENCY EXIT   1060

1063   1062

1065   1064

Imagine that a fire breaks out and you are in Room 1067. Draw the path you would take on the floor plan.

1071   1069   1067

EMERGENCY EXIT

FIRE ALARM BOX   ELEVATOR

1072   1070   1068   1066

11

6 Being a good observer

A police officer is questioning a witness to a robbery. Check (√) the photographs of the man and woman she describes. Make lists of the words that helped you with your choices, one list for the man and one for the woman.

Man	Woman

Match the excerpts from the newspaper stories with the photographs
by writing the correct number beside each picture.

1 But if there is a hero among all those
other heroes and villains, it is Bob
Edgar, the man who has preserved
this historic pocket of the Old West
for all who wish to stop by and see it.

2 White, who worked at a new-car
dealership at the time, said he
needed a gimmick to set himself
apart from the other Bobs there. "If
you go into a showroom and ask for
Bob, you'll get three guys," he says.
After he added the word "beautiful,"
White's car sales doubled, he says.

3 She says she didn't know what she
was getting into when, as a bus
driver, she ran for her first union
leadership post, but now Sandra
White is guiding a local fast
approaching a strike deadline.

4 A steamed-up group turned out in
bone-chilling temperatures yesterday
to protest what they call pornography
on pay TV.

On a separate sheet of paper,
write a short description of the
remaining photograph.

13

7 Watching the weather

A weatherman gives the forecast on the TV evening news. Write the predicted weather conditions for the weekend on the map next to the name of the city.

THE WEATHER

Everyone talks about the weather. Mentioning the weather is a way to greet someone you pass on the street. It's a way to begin a conversation with someone you don't know at a social event. Conversations about the weather are never very long; they are usually only openers to other subjects. A comment about a nice day or a personal complaint about the rain is an easy way to break the ice. Here are some comments about the weather.

Nice day, isn't it?

Hot enough for you?

Looks like rain to me.

A little on the cool side, isn't it?

I wish this rain would stop.

It's a perfect day for staying inside!

I can't stand it. It's freezing!

This rain hasn't let up for two weeks. I'm going crazy!

Gee, it's slippery out there.

Isn't it beautiful out today.

Choose an appropriate comment from the list (or make up one of your own) and write it in the space under each cartoon.

_____

_____

_____

_____

_____

_____

8 Apartment hunting

A man phones a building superintendent for information about an apartment for rent. Fill in the answers to his questions on the checklist.

Call about apt. in <u>Gazette</u>

No. bedrooms:
Rent:
Includes
    heat?
    electricity?
What floor:
Elevator?
Washers/dryers in bldg.?
Near shopping?
Quiet bldg.?
Address:
Who to see:
Time:
Other info:

Read the housing ads and the notices for roommates. Then choose one of the places and write a notice advertising for a roommate to share it with you.

West Side. Lrg sunny 1 BR apt. Kitchen, bath. 2 flr walkup. $400 + 1 mo sec dep. Immediate occ.

DOWNTOWN. Furn 2 BR apt w/ kitchen, din rm, 1 bath. W/w crpt, frplc, balc. Elevator bldg. Avail 3/1. $700 + util. 679-9842 eves.

Bedford. 4½ rm apt. Nr transp + shops. Avail immediately. $300 including util. 481-8769.

NEAR UNIVERSITY: Small 2-rm apt w/bath. No pets or children. Laun in basement. Quiet. $250. 323-1465 anytime.

Sunnyside. 2-story, 3 BR house avail for Feb occ. 2 baths, liv rm, din rm, kitchen. Indoor pkng avail. 40 min to center of town. $900/mo. 524-1773.

ROOMMATE WANTED

Responsible professional woman seeks woman to share rent and utilities of 5½ rm., 2 bath apt., Fisher St. area. No pets. Rent $350. Phone Gloria (after 5) 784-6321

HOUSE TO SHARE

Male grad student, non-smoker, is looking for 2 roommates to share old East Side house. Modern kitchen and baths. Quiet, residential neighborhood, near bus. $230/mo + util.

Glenn 576-9856 (keep trying!)

Now write your own notice.

ABBREVIATION KEY*

apt	apartment	liv rm	living room
avail	available	lrg	large
bath	bathroom	min	minute
balc	balcony	mo	month
bldg	building	nr	near
BR	bedroom	occ	occupancy
crpt	carpet	pkng	parking
din rm	dining room	rm	room
eves	evenings	sec dep	security deposit
flr	floor	transp	transportation
frplc	fireplace	util	utilities
furn	furnished	w/	with
laun	laundry	w/w	wall to wall

*Periods are normally used with abbreviations (e.g., apt.), but in advertisements such as these, they are often omitted.

9 Finding out what's going on in town

Three friends are discussing what movie to see. Fill in the missing information in the ads. Then complete the note to John.

Theater:

THE EMPIRE STRIKES BACK

A LUCASFILM

Times:
Ticket price:

Casablanca

Theater:

Times:

Ticket price:

Theater:

Rocky III

Directed by
Sylvester Stallone

Times:
Ticket price:

Theater:

KRAMER vs. Kramer

Columbia Pictures
Starring
Dustin Hoffman and
Meryl Streep

Times:
Ticket price:

John—
We're going to see _____ at _____ p.m. at the
_____ Theater. Meet us at the Sunset Bar
and Grill (across the street) at _____ p.m. or outside the
theater at _____.

See you later,
Susan, Cindy, Bob

Read the information below. Pick out which concert or concerts you would like to attend and fill out the ticket order form.

The Beethoven Festival

The Nine Symphonies

Wed June 15 8:30 PM
"Leonore" Overture No. 3
Violin Concerto
Symphony No. 1

Sat June 18 8:30 PM
Symphony No. 2
Symphony No. 3, "Eroica"

Fri June 24 8:30 PM
Sat June 25 8:30 PM
Symphony No. 4
Symphony No. 5

Wed June 29 8:30 PM
Symphony No. 6, "Pastoral"
Symphony No. 7

Fri July 1 8:30 PM
Sat July 2 8:30 PM
Symphony No. 8
Symphony No. 9, "Choral"

The String Quartets

Fri June 17 8:30 PM
Quartet in A, Op. 18, no. 5
Quartet in F, Op. 59, no. 1
Quartet in C-sharp minor, Op. 131

Sun June 19 8:30 PM
Quartet in E-flat, Op. 127
Quartet in E-flat, Op. 18, no. 2
Quartet in E minor, Op. 59, no. 2

Tues June 21 8:30 PM
Quartet in F, Op. 18, no. 1
Quartet in A minor, Op. 132
Quartet in C, Op. 59, no. 3

Thurs June 23 8:30 PM
Quartet in C minor, Op. 18, no. 4
Quartet in B-flat, Op. 130

Sun June 26 8:30 PM
Quartet in D, Op. 18, no. 3
Quartet in F minor, Op. 95
Quartet in F, Op. 135

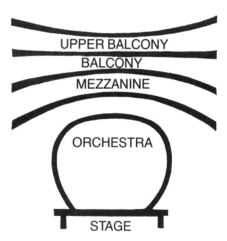

UPPER BALCONY
BALCONY
MEZZANINE
ORCHESTRA
STAGE

Date	Section	# Tickets	Price		Total
June 15	_____	_____	$ _____	=	$ _____
June 17	_____	_____	$ _____	=	$ _____
June 18	_____	_____	$ _____	=	$ _____
June 19	_____	_____	$ _____	=	$ _____
June 21	_____	_____	$ _____	=	$ _____
June 23	_____	_____	$ _____	=	$ _____
June 24	_____	_____	$ _____	=	$ _____
June 25	_____	_____	$ _____	=	$ _____
June 26	_____	_____	$ _____	=	$ _____
June 29	_____	_____	$ _____	=	$ _____
July 1	_____	_____	$ _____	=	$ _____
July 2	_____	_____	$ _____	=	$ _____
			GRAND TOTAL	=	$ _____

_____ Check enclosed

_____ VISA _____ MasterCard _____ American Express

_____ Exp. _____

Name _____ Day Phone _____

Address _____

City _____ State _____ Zip _____

Ticket Prices

Orchestra	$20.00
Mezzanine, rows A-E	20.00
Mezzanine, rows F-K	15.00
Balcony	10.00
Upper Balcony	7.00

10 Finding out about a course

A student phones a college office for information about courses.
Write down the answers to her questions.

Things to do – Aug. 29

Call Clarkson College about computer programming courses – TODAY!

Name of course:
Which evening(s)?
Time:
Dates: Starts –
Ends –

Cost:

Registration
When:
Where:
What to bring:

Janet Morgan is looking for a job. Choose the best job for her and give your reasons.

HELP WANTED

KITCHEN HELP

Casa Theresa, Mexican restaurant, has immediate openings for kitchen help. Day shift only. No experience required, will train. Excellent benefits. Apply in person 2–4 p.m., Mon. through Thurs.

> CASA THERESA
> 1436 Midland Dr.
> Equal Opportunity Employer

OPPORTUNITY

To work at Watchdog Security Corp. as a guard. Night shift, 12 a.m. to 8 a.m. We offer free uniforms, paid vacations, and yearly bonus. If you are intelligent and mature, and have a car, phone, and clean police record, apply Mon.–Fri. in person at 487 North Ave., Suite 318.

PROGRAMMER

Entry level, to $20,000. Must have knowledge of data processing and COBOL. Hours 8:30 a.m. to 5 p.m. Many benefits. Call Barney Reese at 555-4996 (agency).

RECEPTIONIST

Attractive and personable individual wanted to work in glamorous, busy modeling agency. Office skills not essential. Must be prepared to work 2 evenings and Saturdays. Sunday and Monday off. Must be able to handle pressure situations.
> NORMA STEEL STUDIOS
> Call Ms. Tompkin 555-7159

RECEPTIONIST/TYPIST

Private school. We are seeking a mature candidate, able to handle a variety of office routines. Must type 55 wpm. Knowledge of word processors or willingness to train in this area a must. Apply in writing only, giving details of experience and references, to:
> Mrs. M. Forman
> St. Michael's School
> 423 Mohawk Rd.
> Rockford, IL 61107

EMPLOYMENT WANTED

Woman with two school-age children seeks employment. Typing 60 wpm and shorthand. References. Tel.: 784-2953.

Which is the best job for Janet Morgan? Why?

11 Talking about television

Two friends are talking about television. Put a check (✓) in the appropriate box to indicate which programs Dave watched and which programs Nancy watched.

Write the name of the program and the channel number under each picture. If you don't hear the channel number, write "not mentioned."

☐ Dave   ☐ Nancy

Name of program: _____

_____

Channel: _____

☐ Dave   ☐ Nancy

Name of program: _____

_____

Channel: _____

☐ Dave   ☐ Nancy

Name of program: _____

_____

Channel: _____

☐ Dave   ☐ Nancy

Name of program: _____

_____

Channel: _____

Here are some examples of different types of programs. What types do you like? Fill in the questionnaire.

TV QUESTIONNAIRE

1. Do you like these types of programs?

	YES	NO
Movies		
News and current affairs		
Talk shows		
Sports		
Situation comedies		
Dramatic series		
Soap operas		
Police shows		
Documentaries		
Music		
Game shows		
Cartoons		

2. What is your favorite program?

3. What is your least favorite program?

4. What kinds of programs would you like to see more of?

5. What kinds of programs would you like to see less of?

Police show:
Hill Street Blues

Situation comedy:
M*A*S*H

Dramatic series:
DALLAS

Sports:
Wide World of Sports

Music:
Late Night Video

Talk show:
The Tonight Show

Documentary:
Wild Wild World of Animals

News & current affairs:
The 11 o'Clock News

Cartoon:
Mickey Mouse

Soap opera:
General Hospital

Game show:
The Price Is Right

23

12 Running errands

Norm has offered to run some errands for his friend, Sandy. On the shopping list, write the places where Norm can find the items. Label the positions of these places on the map.

shopping list

1 loaf bread – Cantor's
3 lbs. apples –
1 lb. cheddar cheese –
5 lb. box rice –
2 lbs. coffee –
1 qt. milk –
6-pack Coke –
large tube toothpaste –

Registered letter –

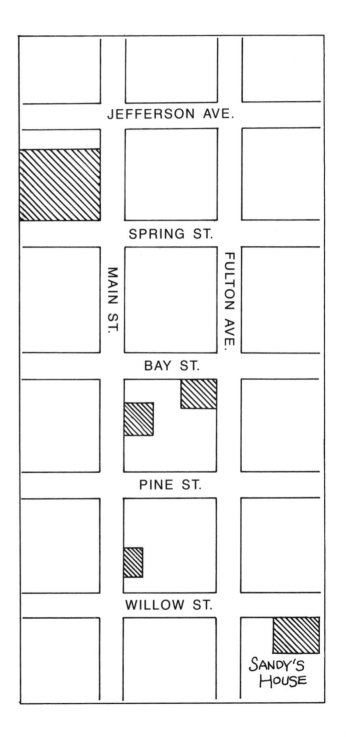

How much will these groceries cost?

$1.89 each

Domino Pure cane SUGAR GRANULATED

$1.19 2 lbs.

2 pineapples ____
4 bars soap ____
1 box sugar ____
2 dozen eggs ____
1 lb. butter ____
2 cans diet Coke ____

total ____

$1.15 dozen

60¢ 12-oz. can

diet Coke Less than 1 Calorie 12 FL OZ 354 mL

39¢ lb.

White Rose Enriched Thin No. 9 Spaghetti.

65¢ lb.

Now make up your own shopping list and work out how much your groceries will cost.

$2.09 lb.

White Rose LIGHTLY SALTED Creamery **butter** NET WT. 16 OZ (1 LB.) 454 GRAMS

Lindsay California **Pitted** Green Ripe Olives **Large** net dr. wt. 6 oz.

$1.05 6-oz. can

IVORY SOAP

40¢ bar

13   Phoning a service station

A customer phones a service station to find out
what is wrong with her car. Fill in the
information about the car in the chart below.

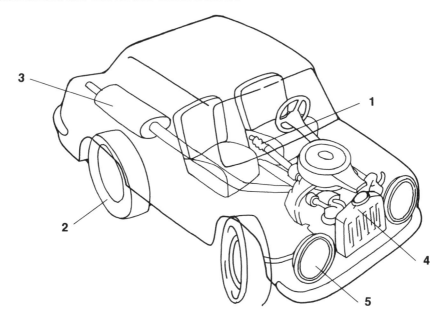

Part of car	OK	Needs attention	Notes
1 emergency brake			
2 tires			
3 muffler			
4 radiator			
5 headlights			

Check the amount that the
mechanic guesses the
repairs will cost:

☐ $400 or less
☐ exactly $400
☐ more than $400

Which car do you think is best for the Patterson family and why?
Which car would you choose for yourself? Give reasons.

Mr. and Mrs. Patterson live in the suburbs of Seattle, Washington. They have three children, ages 7, 9, and 13. Mrs. Patterson drives her husband to work near their home. Then she takes the children to school and drives to her job in the city.

They always use a car for family vacations. The Pattersons like to ski in the winter and go camping in the summer.

Jeep Cherokee Chief

Gas: 19 mpg
Large car that specializes in rough roads and long trips. Very roomy, plenty of luggage space, both inside and on top of car. Practical for recreational use.

Dodge Aries 4-Door

Gas: 26 mpg
Front and back seats each hold 3 people. Roomy trunk. Has trouble on very rough roads, but otherwise gives a smooth, quiet ride. Very likable medium-sized car.

Toyota Tercel Liftback

Gas: 36 mpg
Small but spacious car. Back seat holds 2 people comfortably. Very reliable on both rough and smooth roads. Small amount of luggage space behind back seat.

Chevrolet Corvette

Gas: 16 mpg
Sporty small car, fun to drive. Fast and easy to handle, with quick acceleration and good braking. Moderate noise level. Comfortable front seats.

The Pattersons

My choice

14 Moving in

A young couple is moving into a small apartment. Write the name of each piece of furniture in its correct position on the floor plan.

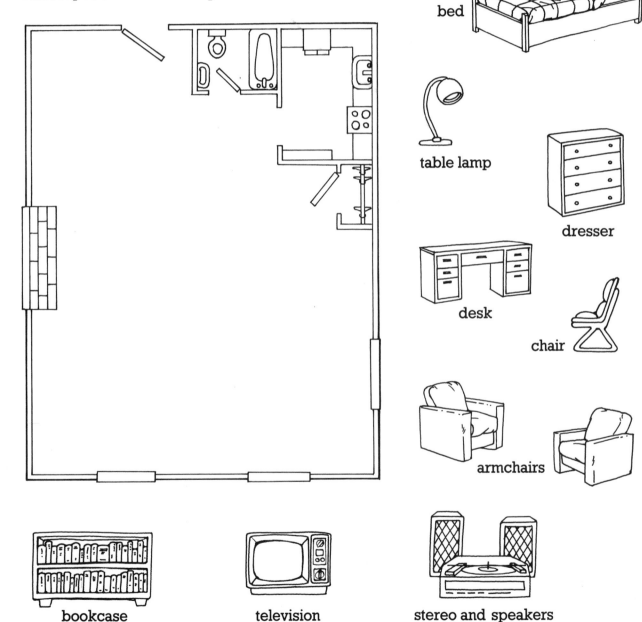

bed

table lamp

dresser

desk

chair

armchairs

bookcase

television

stereo and speakers

Choose three items and order them for Rod and Sophia Carter's new home. Their address is 46 Calvert St., Apt. 2, Baltimore, Maryland 21225.

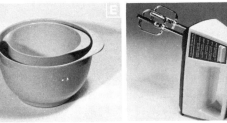

A **Stainless Steel Cookware.** 3-Piece set. 1 quart saucepan, 1 cup saucepan, and 6″ frying pan.
F3900 **$34.50**

B **Wine Glasses.** Set of 4. Each glass holds 12 ounces.
F4215 **$31.99**

C **Ceramic Teapot.** Holds 2 cups. Light green, sky blue, or rose.
F8672 **$6.95**

D **Pepper Grinder and Salt Shaker.** Set. 6″ high. Dark wood only.
G1113 **$7.99**

E **Mixing Bowls.** 2-Piece set consists of 2½ quart and 1½ quart plastic bowls. Bright yellow, orange, or brown.
G4963 **$9.89**

F **General Electric Light'n Easy® Self Clean II™ Iron.** Steam or dry iron, with built-in sprinkling system for dampening wrinkles. Tan with brown accents or white with black accents.
M7711 **$29.99**

G **General Electric 5-Speed Mixer.** 5-Speed fingertip control. Tan, harvest gold, white.
L6224 **$25.99**

H **General Electric Automatic Drip Coffeemaker.** Built-in clock and timer. Coffeemaker turns on at whatever time is pre-set. Makes from 2 to 10 cups.
M7889 **$59.99**

Designs, Inc., Aspen, Colorado

Ordered by (please print):

Ship to (if different from address on left):

First Name	Middle Initial	Last Name
Street		
City	State	Zip Code

First Name	Middle Initial	Last Name
Street		
City	State	Zip Code

Catalogue No.	Quantity	Color	Description	Price	
			TOTAL		

29

15 Handling an emergency

A swimming instructor is demonstrating artificial respiration for two students. Put the pictures in the correct order by writing the number in the box in each picture. Then complete the sentences underneath the pictures.

Check for breathing. Listen at the _____ and _____.

Make a tight seal over the _____.

Give the first _____ as quickly as possible.

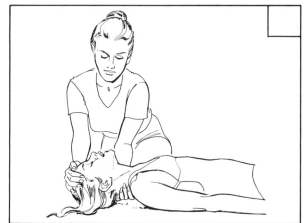

Lift the _____ from behind and press down on the _____.

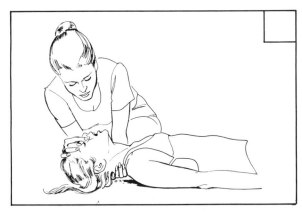

Pinch the _____ and keep _____ on the forehead.

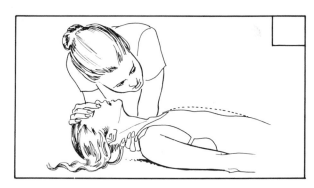

Breathe every _____ seconds and check if the _____ is falling.

Read the excerpt from a magazine article interview with professional burglar Sticky Fingers. Then complete the tips on how to avoid having your home burglarized.

Better Safe than Sorry

THE BEST WAY to handle an emergency is to avoid one, if you can. Part Four of our ongoing series on crime prevention focuses on protecting your home against burglary. Sticky Fingers, an experienced burglar now serving a 6-year prison sentence, agreed to talk to our reporter.

Reporter: Sticky, what do you look for before burglarizing a house?
Fingers: Well, first, I make sure no one is home and no one is watching. I nose around neighborhoods where people don't seem to know each other very well. That way, I won't be noticed. Next, I try to find a house where the people are on vacation and not likely to return soon. I do this by looking for houses with no lights on in the evening. Then I look at doorways. They're a sure giveaway. When newspapers, mail, and deliveries are piled up, I can tell that people have been away for days. I can even count how many days from the number of newspapers.

Reporter: How do you break into a house?
Fingers: Well, usually it's no sweat. Lots of times people leave a window open, or doors and windows unlocked. Then I just slip in. When I have to break in, I look for a patio door on the first floor. They usually

have weak locks and you can force them easily. I watch out for dogs, though. If I hear a dog barking, I go somewhere else.

PROTECT YOUR HOME!

1. Get acquainted with your _____.

2. Be sure to _____ your windows and _____ them.

3. Before leaving for vacation, stop delivery of _____

   and _____.

4. Leave at least one _____ on while you are _____.

5. Strengthen the _____ on your patio door.

6. Get a mean-sounding _____.

16 Making travel plans

A customer is talking with his travel agent. Fill in the missing information (not all of the information can be filled in). Which travel plan do you think is best for him?

Weekend Special

Fare _____

Leaves Detroit on _____ at _____

Arrives in Miami at _____

Leaves Miami on _____ at _____

Arrives in Detroit at _____

7-Day Excursion

Fare _____

Leaves Detroit on _____ at _____

Arrives in Miami at _____

Leaves Miami on _____ at _____

Arrives in Detroit at _____

Night Flight

Fare _____

Leaves Detroit on _____ at _____

Arrives in Miami at _____

Leaves Miami on _____ at _____

Arrives in Detroit at _____

Read the advertisements below and choose one of the places for your vacation.

HYATT REGENCY MAUI

The Hyatt Regency Maui on Kaanapali Beach offers a rare blend of stylish elegance with the best that is Hawaii: breathtaking beauty, balmy breezes, and aloha-spirited people.

- Air-conditioned rooms
- Nearby lakes and waterfalls
- Tennis and golf
- Sailing, snorkeling, swimming
- Variety of elegant shops
- Gourmet restaurants & lounges
- Disco
- Friendly staff

Sequoia National Forest

Sequoia National Forest campsites in California offer a relaxing wilderness experience for people who want to escape the routines of daily life. Enjoy the solitude – your only neighbors will be trees, squirrels, and maybe a few deer!

- Magnificent scenery
- Variety of hiking trails
- Shower & toilet facilities
- Rivers
- Boat rentals
- Fishing
- Campfire sites
- Picnic tables

Now write a postcard to a friend about your vacation. Describe what the place is like and what you are doing. (Use a separate piece of paper, if you wish.)

PLACE STAMP HERE

17   Renting a car

A man phones a car rental agent about renting a car. Fill in the information on his checklist.

Car rental

U-Drive-It : 481-8862
Leave Friday July 7 and return
   Monday July 10

Best car for family of 3 & camping
   equipment:
Standard or automatic?
Pick up at what time?
Return by?

Rates:
Special weekend rate?
Mileage rate?

Insurance included?
   If no, how much?
Deposit?
Other?

IF YOU ARE INVOLVED IN AN ACCIDENT

1. STOP. Failure to stop at the scene of an accident where your vehicle caused injury or death makes you a hit-and-run driver, subject to severe penalties.

2. Identify yourself and show your driver's license and registration card to the other driver or persons involved, or to any police officer.

3. Notify local law authorities or a police officer if anyone is injured.

4. Report the accident to the local police and to the Department of Motor Vehicles. Also report the accident to your insurance company.

5. If you hit a parked vehicle or damage other property, try to find the owner and identify yourself before you leave the scene. If you can't find the owner, leave a note with your name and address and notify the local police.

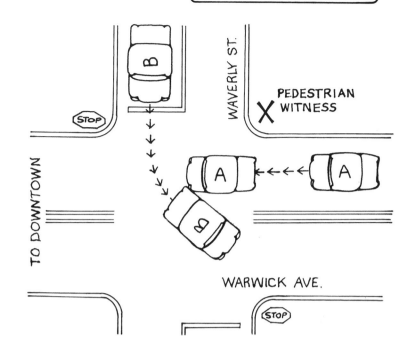

The drivers of the cars in the accident above should:

1. _____

2. _____

_____

_____

_____

3. _____

_____

_____

4. _____

_____

_____

_____

Write a report of the accident as seen from the position of the pedestrian witness.

18 Fitting in an appointment

An actress and her secretary are trying to fit an appointment into a busy schedule. Fill in the times of the appointments. Cross out appointments that are being changed and write in the new ones.

2 Monday April

6 a.m.	makeup session
_____	filming
_____	lunch w/agent
_____	fashion designer
_____	hairdresser
_____	dinner-newspaper columnist

3 Tuesday April

_____	photography session
_____	graduation luncheon - speech
_____	publisher
_____	rehearsal-TV show
_____	
_____	

4 Wednesday April

6 a.m.	makeup session
8 a.m.- 3:30 p.m.	filming
_____	
_____	
_____	
_____	

Fill in George Thompson's appointments for the week of the 23rd.

MON	
23	
TUE	
24	
WED	
25	
THUR	
26	
FRI	
27	
SAT	
28	
SUN	
29	

THUR October 26

WEST SIDE STORY

8:00 p.m.
Miami Beach Community Theater
50 Coconut Ave.

THUR October 26

ST E RY

p.m.
ni Beach
munity
ter
oconut Ave.

Sun. a.m.

George - Dropped by but you were out. Come by for some wine & cheese this afternoon at 4, if you can. Peter's coming, too.
XXX Bonnie

Mr. and Mrs. Frank A. Walters
request the pleasure of your
company
at the marriage of their daughter
Nancy
and
Mario Valenza
Saturday, the twenty-eighth of
October
at half past four o'clock
at the home of
Mr. and Mrs. Frank A. Walters
3015 Flamingo Circle
Miami, Florida 33166

R.S.V.P.

To _Mr. Thompson_
Date _10/23_ Time _1:00 p.m._

WHILE YOU WERE OUT
Ms. _Mika Sadai_
of _Sadai Associates_
Phone _305-8493_
 Area Code   Number   Extension

TELEPHONED		PLEASE CALL	
CALLED TO SEE YOU		WILL CALL AGAIN	
WANTS TO SEE YOU		URGENT	
	RETURNED YOUR CALL	X	

Message _She will bring contracts on Wednesday at 9:30 a.m._

Ann
Operator

APPOINTMENT
George Thompson
on _Oct 27_ at _10:00 a.m._

KIM WU, M.D.
25 Heron Ave., Rm. 602
Miami, Florida 33166
Telephone: 305-9824

CALL 24 HOURS BEFORE IF YOU
CAN'T KEEP APPOINTMENT.

19 Learning how to use a machine

The landlady is showing a new tenant the laundry room. Mark where the clothes and detergent go. Where is the water temperature dial? Where is the dial for type of wash? Where is the coin slot? Label them on the picture.

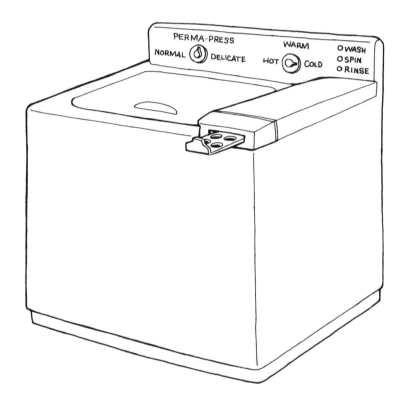

Now write the water temperatures the landlady suggests for the different types of wash.

Type of wash	Temperature
whites	Hot
colors	C
perma-press	warm
delicates	warm
woolens	C

How to operate a photocopier

The copier makes two sizes of copy: 8½ × 11 inches (letter size) or 8½ × 14 inches (legal size). Pushing one of the buttons on the far right of the panel selects the paper size.

The sheet to be copied is placed face down on the glass plate and the cover is closed. The number of copies is selected by pushing the buttons on the left side of the panel. The big rectangular button that says "Normal" is pushed to start copying. Pushing the smaller buttons below makes the copy darker or lighter.

Copies come out onto the tray on the right of the machine.

Write the instructions you would give someone making photocopies for the first time. Use the key phrases to help you.

Key phrases

push button / face down / select number / on the far right / on the left side

20 Sightseeing

Look at pictures 1–6. They are photographs of places of interest in Washington, D.C. Listen to the tour guide and put the number of the picture in the correct location on the map (the guide does not mention one of the places).

1. The White House

2. The National Gallery

3. The Capitol

4. Lincoln Memorial

5. Washington Monument

6. National Air & Space Museum

Now listen again and match these descriptions to the pictures. Write the description in the space under the picture.

a. dedicated to first U.S. president
b. has exhibits on the space age
c. home of U.S. presidents

d. has European and American art
e. burned by British in War of 1812
f. built in honor of President Lincoln

Read this letter to the San Francisco Convention and Visitors Bureau.
Where is the sender's address? Where is the date? What kind of
punctuation is used in the date? in the opening? in the closing?

2-17-3 Kamitsuruma
Setagaya-Ku
Tokyo (6), Japan
February 2, 1990

San Francisco Convention &
  Visitors Bureau
201 3rd St., Suite 900
San Francisco, CA 94103 U.S.A.

Dear Sir or Madam:

My family and I are planning to visit San Francisco
in April. I would appreciate it if you would send
me information about hotel accommodations and
restaurants as well as information on places of
interest and sightseeing tours. I would also
appreciate information on places in the area where
we can go camping.

Thank you very much for your help.

Sincerely,

Tsunemichi Watanabe

Tsunemichi Watanabe

On a separate sheet of paper, write (or type) a letter to the
Washington Convention and Visitors Association, 1575 I Street N.W.,
Washington, D.C. 20005, U.S.A. Ask for information about hotels,
places of interest, transportation, or whatever you want to know.